THE
SHAME RESPONSE
TO REJECTION

Herbert E. Thomas, M.D.

Dedication

TO

R. Rabinovich

AND THE

Munkacs Community,

AN ASSIGNMENT.

I said I will become wise,
but it is far from me.

Ecclesiastes 7:23

Copyright© 1997 by Herbert E. Thomas.

All rights reserved under International and Pan-American Copyright Conventions. Published in the United States by
ALBANEL PUBLISHERS, SEWICKLEY, PENNSYLVANIA.

Library of Congress Catalogue Card Number: 97-94278
ISBN 0-9659920-0-4

35798642
Printed in the United States of America on acid-free paper.

First Edition — 1997

PREFACE

The purpose of presenting this small volume to the reader is to inform him or her of how the experience of rejection may cause a primitive physiological response, a physical response, in his or her body. I have termed it the shame response. Learning the elements of rejection and understanding its consequence to the body allows us to see how rejection manifests itself in human relations.

Those who cannot recall experiencing a shame response, as described herein, will have difficulty believing that it can be one of the most painful of human emotions. Having been loved and accepted has given them a quality of life that many have never known, not even in dreams.

I wish to thank Herbert C. Thomas, my son, for editing this work.

Herbert E. Thomas, M. D.

SEWICKLEY, PENNSYLVANIA
JULY 15, 1997

TABLE OF CONTENTS

I.	OBJECTIFICATION	1
II.	REJECTION	5
III.	SHAME	11
IV.	THE SHAME RESPONSE	15
V.	VULNERABILITY	23
VI.	THE SHAME RESPONSE AND VIOLENCE	29
VII.	THE SHAME RESPONSE AND CULTURAL ISSUES	35
VIII.	HEALING	41
IX.	ACCEPTANCE	45
X.	EQUALITY	49
	REFERENCES	53

I

OBJECTIFICATION

From sodden plains in West and East the blood of kindly men streams up in mists of hate polluting Thy clean air: and nations great in reputation of the arts that bind the world with hopes of heaven, sink to state of brute barbarians, whose ferocious mind gloats over the bloody havoc of their kind, not knowing love or mercy.

Robert Palmer
(Killed in action; January 21, 1916)[1]

World War I is a watershed in the history of Western Civilization. It cast an indelible mark on our collective memory. There is no going back to Edwardian or Victorian times, when man and his inventions were seen as working together for the advancement of civilization.

During the "Great War," as it was known, the generals and many of their senior staff were further removed from the scenes of actual fighting than in any previous war. Long range artillery bombardments often forced them to remain twenty-five miles or more behind the front lines. Senior staff officers rarely visited with troops who, at times, were so close to the enemy that they could actually overhear conversations in the opposing trenches. One senior officer who did visit looked out over a sea of mud and reacted with utter disbelief that anyone could be ordered to fight an enemy in a place where thousands simply drowned.

John Ellis has written a book about the battles in Northern France that took place from 1914 to 1918. "Eye-Deep in Hell" is an effort to capture the essence of four years of trench warfare.[2]

As he suggests, death as an inevitability for millions of soldiers was assumed. Ellis quotes Guy Chapman:

> Hump your pack and get a move on. The next hour, man, will bring you three miles nearer your death. Your life and your death are nothing to these fields — nothing, no more than it is to the man planning the next attack at G.H.Q. You are not even a pawn.

Ellis also quotes a German machine gunner who wrote of a British attack on the Somme:

> We were very surprised to see them walking, we had never seen that before... The officers went in front. I noticed one of them walking calmly, carrying a walking stick. When we started firing we just had to load and reload. They went down in their

hundreds. You didn't have to aim, you just fired into them.

Man seeing man as only an object has ancient roots. The industrial revolution and its need for mass labor followed serfdom which, in turn, had followed slavery. The suddenness, however, with which millions of men were swept away was a trauma for our civilization to bear unlike any we had experienced up to that time. (Using patriotism to rationalize the slaughter simply forged a new tool for future dictators to wield over their people. In World War II, the massive and deliberate bombing of refugees who choked the highways of France in 1940 while attempting to flee the oncoming German tanks was generally accepted as a new and appropriate strategy of war.)

In our own time it would appear that the overhanging threat of nuclear destruction, along with fear of chemical and biological warfare, has checkmated the passions of the militarists in the great powers, at least for the moment. Even so, mass murder in Vietnam, Cambodia, Bosnia and Rwanda remind us of the ever present human propensity to treat others as objects. The total obscenity of such killing fields is cause for despair, as all have occurred since Hiroshima and Nagasaki were destroyed; yet this simple fact that we treat others as objects seems to escape the majority of us.

The objectification of our fellow man reached a peak during the Holocaust, when six million people were condemned to die the most horrible deaths imaginable. Posing no military threat whatsoever, the great majority of victims, unwilling to carry arms out of respect for the laws of Moses, were destroyed simply because they existed.

We qualify the commandment against murder. We abide by its injunction against killing those we know, but at the same time find it quite permissible to kill those we deem to be strangers. Only by objectifying those killed, only by taking from them their humanity, can we protect ourselves against the guilt their deaths would otherwise occasion. In other words, objectification may well be the readiest means at our disposal for assuaging guilt.

II

REJECTION

The last noun in The Trial: "shame". Its last image: the faces of two strangers, close by his own face, almost touching it, watching K,s most intimate state, his death throes. In that last noun, in that last image is concentrated the entire novel's fundamental situation: ...no longer being his own man; losing his status as an individual. The transformation of a man from subject to object is experienced as shame.

Milan Kundera (1993)[3]

"Rejection," as surprising as it may seem, is not considered to be a psychological term. When it does appear in a behavioral science context, it is used in the same way it would be used in everyday conversation. One reads of a parent rejecting a child or a family rejecting one of its members. At times, "scapegoating" is used to describe the rejection of a member of a family, but this word also has an everyday meaning. It, too, has no particular psychological definition. The fact is that "rejection" is seldom used and, when it is, rarely given much importance.

To reject has been defined as "to cast off" (as a person), to forsake.[4] It has been associated with words such as "snub," "rebuff," "repel," "refuse," and "repulse." None of these suggests any particular psychological meaning, nor are they a feature of psychological studies. What precedes the act of rejection, as well as what follows it, is the subject of inquiry, as is scapegoating, but not rejection itself.

Although largely ignored by the field of psychology, the act of rejection had figured prominently in the literature of Western Civilization. A number of key literary works written prior to 1900 actually turn on acts of rejection. Since the publication in 1900 of Sigmund Freud's study of the meaning of dreams,[5] however, an emerging psychology for many novelists has often been that of the unconscious, namely, metapsychology. The novel "Ulysses" by James Joyce[6] is one such example, in that he depends heavily on the idea of free association, a classic Freudian concept.

In one of the most complete descriptions of an act of rejection and its consequences that I have found, Jane Austen, in her novel "Emma,"[7] describes a scene in which the heroine rejects a woman whom she has known all her life. The entire plot of the novel hinges on this rejection, which occurs near the end of the story.

In this scene, during a picnic on Box Hill, Emma rejects a timid, talkative woman, who talks as a way of attempting to gain acceptance, by telling her she talks too much.

"Oh! very well," exclaimed Miss Bates, "then I need not be uneasy. Three things very dull indeed. That will just do for me, you know. I shall be sure to say three dull things as soon as ever I open my mouth, shan't I? — (looking round with the most good-humored dependence on every body's assent) — Do not you all think I shall?"

Emma could not resist.

"Ah! ma'am, but there may be a difficulty. Pardon me — but you will be limited as to number — only three at once."

Miss Bates, deceived by the mock ceremony of her manner, did not immediately catch her meaning; but, when it burst on her, it could not anger, though a slight blush showed that it could pain her.

Miss Bates is clearly pained by this and Emma is reprimanded for her behavior.

While waiting for the carriage, she found Mr. Knightley by her side. He looked around, as if to see that no one were near, and then said,

"Emma, I must once more speak to you as I have been used to do: a privilege rather endured than allowed, perhaps, but I must still use it. I cannot see you acting wrong without a remonstrance. How could you be so unfeeling to Miss Bates? How could you be so insolent in your wit to a woman of her character, age and situation? — Emma, I had not thought it possible."

Emma's response to Mr. Knightley, her most trusted male friend, is defensive. She asserts that Miss Bates probably never realized she was rejected. This is her defense against his own rejection of her for what she has done.

Emma recollected, blushed, was sorry but tried to laugh it off.

"Nay, how could I help saying what I did? Nobody could have helped it. It was not so very bad. I dare say, she did not understand me."

In fact, as Mr. Knightley makes clear, Emma's remarks carried a profound rejection of Miss Bates.

"I assure you she did. She felt your full meaning. She is poor; she has sunk from the comforts she was born to; and, if she live to an old age, must probably sink more. Her situation should secure your compassion. It was badly done, indeed! — You, whom she had known from an infant, whom she had seen grow up from a period when her notice was an honour, to have you now, in thoughtless spirits, and the pride of the moment, laugh at her, humble her — and before her niece, too... and before others, many of whom (certainly *some*,) would be entirely guided by *your* treatment of her."

As the truth of Mr. Knightley's reproach sinks in, Emma is overwhelmed.

She was vexed beyond what could have been expressed — almost beyond what she could conceal. Never had she felt so agitated, mortified, grieved, at any circumstance in her life. She was most forcibly struck. The truth of his representation there was no denying. She felt it at her heart. How could she have been so brutal, so cruel to Miss Bates? — How could she have exposed herself to such ill opinion in any one she valued! And, how suffer him to leave her without saying one word of gratitude, of concurrence, of common kindness!

Time did not compose her. As she reflected more, she seemed but to feel it more. She never had been so depressed.

...Emma felt the tears running down her cheeks almost all the way home, without being at any trouble to check them, extraordinary as they were.

In Charles Dickens' "Great Expectations,"[8] we are introduced to a woman who years earlier experienced a severe rejection on the morning of her wedding day when she learned that her bridegroom had chosen not to attend the ceremony. Her response to this shock was to have all the clocks in her huge house stopped and set to show, for all time, the moment the news arrived. From this point on, the bride, Miss Havisham, also remains frozen in time, living her days in her wedding gown. When she adopts a young girl, Estelle, it is with the avowed purpose of raising her to be a beautiful woman who will win the hearts of men only to then reject them. Miss Havisham's experience of rejection defines the direction the novel will take, for Estelle's rejection of Pip, the story's hero, is crucial to its progress.

In the novel "Frankenstein,"[9] by Mary Wollstonecraft Shelley, a young Swiss scientist creates a monstrous creature in his university laboratory. When this creature is rejected by the only humans he comes to know, his response is anything but monstrous; rather, it is all too human.

> At that instant the cottage door was opened, and Felix, Safie, and Agatha entered. Who can describe their horror and consternation on beholding me? Agatha fainted; and Safie, unable to attend to her friend, rushed out of the cottage. Felix darted forward, and with supernatural force tore me from his father, to whose knees I clung: in a transport of fury, he dashed me to the ground, and struck me violently with a stick. I could have torn him limb from limb, as a lion rends the antelope. But my heart sunk within me as with bitter sickness, and I refrained. I saw him on the point of repeating his blow, when, overcome by pain and anguish, I quitted the cottage, and in the general tumult escaped unperceived to my hovel.

There is no mention of anger by the monstrous creature at any time during the rejection he experiences. The rest of the story, however, describes in great detail how the creature expresses his rage at what has occurred, including his murder of a young boy favored by his creator.

Much earlier than the 19th century, at the beginning of the 17th, a story is told in which a son experiences intense rejection by his mother. It is a play that has captured the imagination of the world ever since. In Shakespeare's "Hamlet,"[10] Hamlet's mother Gertrude hastily marries Hamlet's uncle, whom he despises, following the death of her husband the King. By doing so, she causes Hamlet to experience intense rejection. Well along in the play, he confronts her in her chambers, and she rejects him again, by calling out for help. The intensity of this rejection — her clear lack of trust in her son and her treatment of him as though he were a stranger — is made worse when she cries out her fear that Hamlet could murder her. This prompts Polonius, hidden behind a screen in the room, to call out in response. Because Hamlet thought he was alone with his mother, Polonius' presence seems only to intensify the rejection Hamlet is experiencing. His reaction is to thrust his sword into the hidden Polonius, slaying him.

In this century, the Czech intellectual and novelist Milan Kundera, in his book "Testaments Betrayed,"[11] has written of Franz Kafka's "The Trial" that it is the transformation of an individual from a subject to an object that leads to the experience of shame. This is, I believe, the definition of "rejection": the transformation of a person from subject to object. To say it more succinctly: to reject someone is to objectify them. I further believe that it is the transformation of a person from subject to object that causes one to experience shame, although I choose to define "shame" in a particular way.

III

SHAME

...we can understand the meaning of gestures which accompany blushing throughout the world. These consist in hiding the face, or turning it towards the ground, or to one side. The eyes are generally averted or are restless, for to look at the man who causes us to feel shame or shyness, immediately brings home in an intolerable manner the consciousness that his gaze is directed on us.

Charles Darwin (1873)[12]

Shame is an emotion and not a thought or an idea, although thoughts can be associated with shame, just as thoughts are associated with anger or love. The definition of an emotion is relatively straightforward: it is a *physical* change in the body which affects various systems such as the pulmonary, cardiovascular and musculo-skeletal systems.[13] Because the physical change involves the neuro-endocrine system, emotions can be described as affecting the whole body physically. In addition to shame and anger, other emotions include hate, jealousy, greed and fear, to name only a few.

There is no such agreement as to the definition of shame. At times it is defined as an idea, and at other times as an emotion. Most often, it is defined in terms of what causes it; people say that one was shamed into doing something, as though shame were akin to an appeal to one's better judgment. Elsewhere, shame has been defined as a consciousness of guilt, of a shortcoming, or of a position taken; in other words, it has been intellectualized. As the science of psychology has grown increasingly complex during the course of the twentieth century, theories explaining the causes of shame have increased in number and in complexity, most especially in the last twenty years. Very few, however, have focused on shame as a painful affect state, that is, a painful emotion.

Sigmund Freud first defined shame as an emotion related to aberrations of the sexual instinct, one of the forces restricting the direction taken by the sexual instinct.[14] In such a definition, the cause and the effect are given equal importance. This was considered the explanation of shame in psychoanalytic psychology (metapsychology) until well into the last half of this century when the emergence of other morally forbidden wishes began to be considered as well. The fundamental understanding was that shame flowed from an internal reality and was therefore only indirectly related to others. Interestingly, in an early paper,

Freud referred at least to the possibility of shame involving two individuals and not just one. He wrote: "Feelings of shame in front of other people... are lacking in the melancholic..."[15] Otto Fenichel, a classicist and contemporary of Freud, defined shame as "an archaic physiological response pattern," but he gave no further explanation.[16] It must be assumed, then, that he was describing a response to aberrations of the sexual instinct emerging from the unconscious and that another individual was not considered to be involved in any direct way.

Beginning in the early 1980's, studies on the subject of shame proliferated. Numerous books and articles have appeared, many reflecting a great deal of careful thought. Some of these works focus on shame as something that an individual experiences for reasons within herself or himself. More recently, the focus has turned to shame as it relates to problems in early mother-child relationships. These early one-to-one (dyadic) relationships have been identified by at least one author, Ana-Maria Rizutto, as determining the experience of shame in later life.

Rizutto has written a paper on shame that is both succinct and carefully reasoned. She writes: "Repeated traumatic experiences of being shamed, rejected, slighted in childhood ... leave indelible marks. The emotion experienced in such moments of rejection... is a critical component of the experience of shame in later life."[17]

The trauma Rizutto refers to is physical pain, and the impact it has on the central nervous system is never erased. More importantly, such physical trauma is not limited to childhood.

IV

THE SHAME RESPONSE

She came back, with some bread and meat and a little mug of beer. She put the mug down on the stones of the yard, and gave me the bread and meat without looking at me, as insolently as if I were a dog in disgrace. I was so humiliated, hurt, spurned, offended, angry, sorry — I cannot hit upon the right name for the smart — God knows what its name was — that tears started to my eyes. The moment they sprang there, the girl looked at me with a quick delight in having been the cause of them...

But, when she was gone, I looked about for a place to hide my face in... As I cried, I kicked the wall, and took a hard twist of my hair; so bitter were my feelings, and so sharp was the smart without a name, *that needed counteraction.*

Charles Dickens (1861)[18]

In America, as in most English-speaking countries, we generally assume that when a person is rejected, fired for example, he or she may become angry. We also assume that it is the seriousness of the rejection that determines the degree of anger. Thus, we have an equation with two simple variables.

In fact, the dynamics of rejection are more complex. Frequently, a discreet phenomenon that I refer to as the "shame response,"[19] a primitive physiological (physical) response, is a direct consequence of rejection. It is the shame response, which can be extremely painful, that causes anger. Hence, there are three factors at work, and not just two. Rejection does not cause anger; rejection causes a shame response which *then* causes anger. These three factors or stages of rejection are considered in turn.

REJECTION:

Rejection is, in effect, the communication of an idea, whether verbal or non-verbal. The five separate elements that determine the strength of the rejection are as follows:

A. The significance to the person rejected of the one who rejects. The significance of the one who rejects is readily understood. It may be one's spouse, a close friend, or any person acknowledged as a significant authority in one's life.

B. The significance to the person rejected of those who witness the rejection. Witnesses to the rejection may be held to be significant for similar reasons. Any group to which a person belongs, especially one that possesses elitist pretensions, would be significant.

C. The rejected person's vulnerability to experiencing rejection. Vulnerability to rejection (*see Chapter V*) is related to two factors in particular. The first involves the circumstances under which a person, in the course of his or her development, has separated from significant others and, as a result, has become independent and autonomous. The second is the person's past experiences of rejection, be they real or perceived as real. Whether real or not, the frequency and intensity of the rejections must be considered.

D. Whether what is rejected is an aspect of one's self or of one's whole self. Where the whole self is rejected, rather than just an aspect of self, one is less able to evaluate or measure the rejection. (*This is particularly true of children who are told that they are bad and not that what they did was bad.*)

E. The degree of surprise associated with the rejection. The degree of surprise, perhaps even shock, takes on special significance, for the greater surprise, the less prepared the person will be to deal with the rejection.

These five elements must be considered in any appraisal of a rejection.

SHAME RESPONSE:

The second stage, that of the shame response to the rejection, is an emotional one, yet we can track its presence because so often it manifests itself *physically*.

The shame response can vary greatly in intensity, ranging from mild to severe. People have reported a mild feeling of discomfort in the head to a feeling, especially painful, that the head is about to explode; from a slight blush on the cheeks to a deep reddening of the head and neck and, at times, even the shoulders; from a tightness in the throat to a sense of being choked; from mild nausea and abdominal cramping to vomiting and a sensation that the contents of one's abdomen are about to fall out on the floor; from a tightness in the chest to a feeling of suffocation or, in its most extreme form, a feeling that one's chest is about to explode or implode. Sensations of a shame response can also be more generalized throughout the body and include such feelings as being dazed or stunned.

This second stage, that of the shame response, ends when the person becomes angry. The pain does not recede before the anger however. It can last indefinitely.

ANGER:

The third stage is anger, but the ways in which the anger manifests itself vary greatly. Some turn the anger against themselves, some displace it on to less significant others, and some direct it at the person who has rejected them. Should the anger exceed the threshold of the person's ability to contain it, he or she may become violent. In order to mark this threshold in a particular individual, one needs to consider his or her vulnerability. As noted, individual vulnerability is a function of past experiences of painful rejection and the degree to which the person has become separated from significant others during his or her development. In addition, however, many current factors will influence vulnerability. The presence of alcohol circulating in the blood, the presence of abnormal brain activity, and other organic factors must all be considered if they are present in the person being evaluated. Current medications, such as anti-depressants, need to be accounted for. Also, the amount of stress experienced may cause a person to regress, to become more childlike, and hence more vulnerable.

The energy associated with the anger flowing from a shame response is directly related to the energy associated with the pain of the shame response that precedes it. If anger is discharged through acts of violence, there tends to be a return to the resting state, homeostasis, that was present before the rejection occurred. Where there is no discharge of energy in violent acts, the energy associated with the anger will most likely be directed into one's body. Whether or not the energy associated with the pain of the shame response and the succeeding anger is discharged, the psychic trauma caused by the experienced pain remains. As discussed in the next chapter, when this trauma is severe, it acts as a precipitating factor for post-traumatic phenomena.

At this point, a consideration of why the shame response has not been discovered before now is instructive. Our minds have two principal ways of protecting us from becoming fully aware of the experience of a shame response. Because they have protected us so well, they have also kept us ignorant of the role the shame response plays in our lives.

First, our minds deal with an experience of rejection, and the shame response, by repressing it. In the same way that a vivid dream is lost to recall soon after one awakes, so is the rejection and shame response sequence lost to recall through repression.

Second, we sometimes repress pain but remember the event. This is "isolation," and it is common. It allows one to be aware of the rejection and also one's reaction to it but to avoid a re-experience of the painful feelings the event caused. For example, one can recall being fired and leaving the room where the firing occurred, but not the pain and possibly some of the anger that accompanied it.

Because repression and isolation — both are defense mechanisms — work so efficiently, the shame response has caused much less observable trauma in people's lives than it would have otherwise, but it has also left us ignorant of one of the most important and, at times, most painful of human emotions.

The efficiency with which the mind represses or isolates the shame response, especially when it is particularly painful, is never complete. If we begin to reflect on our responses to past experiences of rejection, this quickly becomes apparent. As we begin to re-experience rejection, we once again seek to repress and isolate. If we are determined to examine such experiences, however, we begin to follow paths that lead to other such experiences. The problems of re-visiting past rejections are manifold, and worthy of a study in and of themselves.

- If we talk seriously of the pain of a past shame response to a rejection, we begin to re-experience the pain.

- If we talk of a past shame response to another, especially one who is significant, we feel at risk of another rejection and become anxious.

- If we talk of a painful shame response, it may recall other painful shame responses by association.

- If we talk of a past shame response, we may realize by association that it has led us to cause others pain.

- Therapists listening to clients recall the experience of a painful shame response may be incapable of further listening for all of the preceding reasons.

Although the shame response has proven elusive until now, the following individuals were able to describe painful shame responses with help from their therapist.

I.

A thirty-six-year-old woman recalled an event that took place in her family's apartment, when she was nine-and-a-half years old. She recounted the event in the course of her therapy with great clarity.

One Saturday morning, rising late from her bed, she walked toward the kitchen only to become aware that her parents were talking about her. She overheard her mother ask her father whether he was aware of any family member ever having been committed to a mental hospital. She interpreted this to mean her mother believed her to be "crazy," and she silently withdrew to her room. There, in order to obtain relief from the overwhelming pain she felt in her chest and abdomen, she climbed into bed and assumed a fetal position.

During the course of the next three years, she raged at her mother, who denied ever thinking of her daughter as "crazy." After several visits to a psychiatrist, the girl was told at the age of twelve-and-a-half that she was going to a hospital for a check-up. Once there, she was interviewed by a psychiatrist who said that, as it was late Friday afternoon, he would see her again Monday. It was a private psychiatric hospital in the mid-1950s. Over the weekend, an older patient befriended her and, learning of her problem of repeated outbursts of anger, urged her to stop them as she would most likely be given a course of electro-convulsive therapy at the hospital. She never expressed anger again and was discharged from the hospital on the Monday. Only in therapy did she reveal the intensity of the pain she had experienced when listening to her mother and father talking about her. Part of her believed she was, in fact, "crazy."

II.

A woman, aged forty-three, in intensive psychotherapy, became enraged at the therapist for having said "the most cruel and cutting remark" she ever could have imagined, "not once but three times." Moreover, she saw no evidence that he was aware of how deeply he had hurt her. What the therapist had said was that, if she behaved at work the way she behaved in the office, it was obvious why she was having problems. His remark was prompted by her angry statements that he did not listen to her, that he had ignored her point of view, that he was a male chauvinist, that he was arrogant, and so on. The therapist interpreted these statements as proof of a negative transference, a re-experiencing of anger at a past significant other. During one session, the woman's anguish and rage so overwhelmed her that the therapist asked her exactly what had occurred between the "cutting remark" and the moment she became aware of her anger. Only then did she describe experiencing in her upper chest a pain so intense that she thought her chest would literally explode outward, leaving a gaping hole.

III.

A young man was working in his pizza shop about nine o'clock one evening. His ex-girlfriend, who had left him for a new boyfriend, dropped by to discuss a bill for furniture they had bought when they had intended to live together. When he learned that the new boyfriend was waiting outside, he ordered her to leave the shop and began drinking malt liquor, which he continued to do for several hours. Because of recent robberies, he carried a gun in the belt of his trousers.

After going home to change his clothes around eleven o'clock, he drove to a swimming pool in the nearby park. The pool was closed, yet he knew it was where his ex-girlfriend and her new boyfriend both worked. He vandalized it, cutting phone wires and throwing poolside furniture into the pool. He next drove to an area where he had parked with her in the past, also in the park, and found the couple sitting on a bench. Approaching them, he entered into a long discussion, with her in particular, about their being together again. After perhaps fifteen minutes, he turned and retraced his steps to his car. As he was doing so, he heard a barely audible remark followed by laughter. Enraged, he drew his pistol, turned and fired at the couple as he approached them, killing the man and wounding her. When later questioned, he described feeling an intense pain in his chest and abdomen immediately following the remark and the ensuing laughter.

V

VULNERABILITY

Jesus said, "Love your brother like your soul, protect that person like the pupil of the eye."

The Gospel of Thomas[20]

A person is vulnerable to rejection to the extent that he or she is capable of reacting to rejection with a shame response. Two factors most affect this vulnerability. The first is one's past history of experiencing shame responses. The second is the manner in which one has separated psychologically from significant others, particularly those of childhood.

Some experiences of rejection are understood by the person being rejected as occurring generally and thus are more easily tolerated. Such experiences can accumulate, however, and reach a level of pain that is not tolerable. This threshold level varies from one person to another. For some people, even a single experience of rejection can trigger a shame response so painful as to be intolerable.

At whatever point this threshold is crossed, once crossed, there can be far-reaching consequences for the individual. Ever afterwards, even a slight rejection can ignite intense pain. To avoid this pain, the person who lives in this state of high vulnerability may withdraw and live a solitary existence. This withdrawal may be to such a degree that in time others see the person as eccentric, the person becomes paranoid, or, when touch with reality is lost, the person is diagnosed psychotic.

In the case of the adolescent, a similar pattern of responding to rejection may also unfold. Gang membership can be understood as a channel for the rage that has resulted from the physical pain of shame responses, at the same time ensuring acceptance by significant others.

The second factor determining vulnerability is the manner in which one has separated from the significant others of childhood in becoming independent and autonomous. There are two problems to be considered. One involves insufficient separation and the other involves separation that occurs prematurely as a defense against further experiences of rejection.

In cases of insufficient separation, those seen as parental authorities are imbued with too much significance, and the potential for an intense experience of rejection at their hands therefore persists. Cases of premature separation involve what can be thought of as pseudo-separation. They are attempts to minimize the significance of such authoritarian figures. In achieving a pseudo-separation, the individual gains some protection from pain, yet the price of protection is a subsequent inability to feel close to others.

In two of the following cases, individuals experienced intolerable rejections. In a third, an individual experienced a relatively mild rejection and was able to resolve it.

CASE A

In this case, separation from the significant other occurred prematurely, and the pain of the shame response was severe and chronic.

A young African American woman was raised by her maternal grandmother to the age of thirteen. She described a happy childhood spent with cousins who were also being raised by the grandmother. She had done well in school, as evidenced by her name being placed on the honor roll. She reported no problems with authority figures, and said she had never felt abused or neglected.

At the age of thirteen, her mother told her that she had to move from her grandmother's house to where the mother and her boyfriend lived. After four months of increasing tension over the issue of "who would give" her orders, her mother beat her with an ironing cord. The beating was so severe that the girl was taken to a hospital where photographs were taken of her wounds. She then returned to her grandmother's house and her mother was formally charged with criminal assault.

As she later described it, the pain of her wounds left as her wounds healed, but the pain inside her chest only left when she began to use crack cocaine at the age of seventeen.

CASE B

In this case, problems of insufficient separation from significant others were present, and the pain of the shame response was truly intolerable.

A Caucasian man was at his work station in a factory when his foreman came up behind him, made explicit homosexual propositions, and then left. Two days later, the foreman returned and made the same remarks. This time, he did not leave, and the worker had to ask him to stop as the worker was becoming upset. The foreman did not stop and instead increased the intensity of his abusive behavior. Because of his fear that he would be fired, the worker did not attempt to leave, despite what he was experiencing inside himself. At first, he experienced pressure in his head that rapidly grew into severe pain. A second pain, experienced in his chest, also steadily increased as the abuse continued. When the pain was no longer tolerable and the worker felt that his head would explode, he found himself suddenly outside his body in an "envelope," surrounded by amorphous shapes of men, all of whom were sexually and sadistically mocking him. The pain was intolerable, yet still it continued to build, until he began to experience flashbacks to traumatic wartime events. At this point, the foreman left.

This man's ability to tolerate pain was limited because of past experiences of rejection in the military which had been intensely painful. In therapy, because he was overwhelmed with pain as he began to recount what had taken place, he was given responsibility for establishing the frequency of his sessions. It was left to him to determine when to terminate a session if the pain was too intense. As he did so, he began to gain some control over what had occurred.

CASE C

In this case, separation had occurred, and the pain of the shame response was mild. Further separation was needed, however, for the pain to fully subside.

A man wrote to his parents saying that his lifestyle was a homosexual one. This was something he had kept a secret from them. After a long wait, in which he became increasingly anxious, a letter arrived from his mother in which she rejected his homosexuality and described it as "disgusting." In therapy, although he initially spoke of his anger at his mother, in time he was able to describe the shame response that he had experienced between the time he read her letter and his becoming angry. When told by the therapist that he needed to understand his mother, he became even angrier. He challenged the right of anyone to tell him not to be angry with her. He was told that he had every right to be angry, but unless he credited her with being a separate and autonomous person, he would not rid himself of the painful shame response he had experienced.

As he described her going to confession everyday, taking flowers and baked goods to the priests' home, he began to reflect on the church's position on homosexuality. The more he felt her to be a separate person, the more the pain subsided. As it did so, his anger towards her also subsided. He was left with a feeling of sadness, knowing that he and his mother would never again experience the closeness that they had shared in the past.

VULNERABILITY:
NEUROLOGICAL CONSIDERATIONS

To fully understand why the accumulated pain of shame responses can affect one so dramatically, it is necessary to understand the neurological basis for it.

It appears that the pain of the shame response acts as a traumatic event, a wounding, as it is located, or stored, in a specific area of the brain, either in the cingulate gyrus or nearby. This area at the base of the brain has been associated with post-traumatic stress phenomena;[21] it is where feelings associated with various traumatic events are stored.

When stimulated by an additional increment of pain, the energy stored in this area can be automatically and rapidly discharged. This phenomenon of a rapid and uncontrolled discharge is the basis of what is termed "kindling." The outward manifestation of kindling can be an outburst of anger or even rage. Many individuals with a history of repeated outbursts resulting from apparently minimal provocation should be seen as suffering from a disease requiring treatment directed at the prevention of kindling. When even small amounts of anti-convulsant medication are used, the phenomenon of kindling may be completely stopped. In a large number of men and women who suffer from periodic rages, the use of such medication stops the kindling, and, hence, they no longer exhibit such outbursts. In many cases, this medication can prevent kindling from occurring in less than half an hour following ingestion when properly diagnosed.

VI

THE SHAME RESPONSE AND VIOLENCE

No matter how glorified or how piously disguised, vengeance as a human motive must be personally repudiated by each and everyone of us.

Karl Menninger [22]

Experiences of abuse and neglect in childhood are often used to explain acts of violence committed in adult life, implying that the anger at having been abused or neglected is discharged years later in the form of violent behavior. If these experiences of abuse and neglect are seen as rejections, however, then we can also see that the anger follows from repeated shame responses. It is the collective pain of these responses that needs to be reckoned with, for it persists unchanged into the present in the mind of the one rejected.

A study done of the medical records of fourteen adolescents condemned to death showed that twelve had suffered brutal physical abuse and five had been sexually abused by relatives.[23] If those assigned to work with these youths give priority to the youth's anger, they are likely to conclude that the youths are incorrigible, for their capacity for anger is deep and its discharge unpredictable. Giving priority to anger will only serve to complicate treatment. Giving priority to their pain, however, acknowledging that it persists and causes their angry outbursts, allows us to see them as injured rather than incorrigible.

If anger and the failure to control it were the principal problem presented by adolescents who commit violent acts, then the only appropriate response by adults would be strict discipline. If the real problem, however, is the pain of accumulated shame responses, then adults must respond with something more than just discipline. Merely to enforce discipline is to cause further rejection. This is not to say that discipline is somehow rendered unnecessary or undesirable, but operating alone it has a negative power.

What is required is a new sensitivity on the part of those in authority. A trusting relationship must be developed in which acts of rejection are carefully, and consciously, avoided. The adolescents described above have a desperate need for acceptance, and this need must be acknowledged. Of course, an announcement to those in authority that they need to relate to adolescents in a way that recognizes their pain, without in any way rejecting or demeaning them, will likely be treated with skepticism. Granted, a world in which authorities charged with the care of violent youth must tiptoe around their charges would soon become unmanageable. But if the focus of care is not merely avoidance of rejection, but active acceptance, then a new path to healing opens.

In the following vignettes, all of which involve adult men, a conscious and deliberate effort to communicate acceptance served to preempt violent acts. In fact, lives depended on these men not experiencing rejection at critical moments.

A. A number of years ago, in a staff cafeteria of a maximum security prison, two senior administrators and a psychiatrist (myself) were sitting at a table when they were approached by an inmate waiter carrying a pot of coffee. He had managed somehow to obtain a chef's hat, adding a comic touch to the setting. With a fresh white shirt, white trousers, a white apron and a white towel folded over his left forearm, he approached the table, smiling and bowing as he offered everyone a cup of coffee. Unknown to him, the conversation at the table, an extremely anxious one, concerned the threat of an imminent riot. In response to his offer, he was showered with a string of curses from one of the senior administrators.

The inmate stopped dead in his tracks. A red flush spread upward from his shirt collar and across his neck and face, and he stared in disbelief at the man who had rejected him. He then backed slowly away from the table and retreated behind the cafeteria counter. I was the psychiatrist at the table, and I was facing him. The other two men had their backs to him. The inmate stared at me and I stared back at him. As we did so, a much shorter man, a steward, approached the inmate and asked him why he was standing there. The inmate placed his large arm around the steward's neck and lifted him off the floor, where he dangled, a cigar in his mouth and his arms hanging by his sides. The steward stared at me and I at him. The inmate stared at me and I at him. With all the energy I could muster, I grinned at both of them as widely as I could, and both men grinned back at me. We knew and trusted one another. After what seemed like a very long time, the inmate lowered the steward to the floor, and the steward shook himself off and went about his business as if nothing had happened. The inmate also went about his work. As for the two administrators, they were unaware of what occurred.

B. One afternoon in a small building inside the walls of a maximum security prison, a number of inmates were gathered for group therapy with a psychiatrist (myself) and a woman psychologist when I was told that someone wanted to see me. Waiting in the hall was an inmate I knew well. He was clearly very disturbed and held a large club in his hand. The man could only repeat over and over: "What are you doing to me?"

I gazed at this man straight in the eyes, showed no emotion whatsoever, and talked quietly about how he was obviously troubled. The man ultimately discharged his anger by throwing the club violently at a wall and turning over several large pieces of furniture. Having thus exploded, he then grew calm and agreed to walk with me to the hospital.

At one point during the violent outburst the level of dangerousness suddenly escalated. This was when another inmate, standing next to me, said, "Now, come on, Dan." The man with the club turned toward him with vastly greater observable anger. Only when I told the other man to mind his own affairs did the man with the club focus again back on me. Because of the tendency for anger to be displaced onto a less significant other, the second man was much more at risk than I was at that moment in time.

C. Several weeks after the events just described, the woman psychologist, who had observed all that occurred outside the group therapy room, found herself in a comparable situation. As she worked in her office in a court psychiatric clinic, a huge man entered her office. The clinic was otherwise deserted. The man announced that if she did not marry him at once, he would throw her out of the window, which was several stories above the street. She promptly stood up to better look directly into his eyes. She then began talking to him, showing no emotion.

It was apparent that the man was psychotic and highly delusional. Realizing that the delusions all related in some way or other to scripture, she explained that she was "betrothed" and thus could not marry him. He was clearly taken aback at this development and, as they talked together, he began to calm down. After what, I am sure, seemed a very long time to her, he turned and left the office. Her careful reflection on his desire to marry her was clearly an acceptance of him.

The violent person quite naturally frightens us. When we are frightened, we, too, experience the chain of rejection, shame response, and anger, to which we are likely to respond with a desire more for vengeance than understanding. The fact that a violent person is violent because he or she is in pain will generally be overlooked, especially if the threat of violence is imminent. In the above examples, however, active acceptance of the potentially violent person, respect for his pain, was crucial to another's survival.

As human beings, we have long puzzled over the roots of violent behavior. Without an understanding of the role of the shame response in the provocation of anger and rage, violent behavior will forever seem random and unpredictable.

In the following case, a particularly vicious murder had long gone unexplained. Many years after he was sent to prison, a man explained for the first time why he had murdered his girlfriend. He said he had killed her because she knew of his preference for certain "unusual" sexual acts. He had become convinced that she was going to leave him and, once she had done so, she would tell their friends about his proclivities. He was certain that, when she did so, they would reject him. That he would destroy her life as well as his own in order to avoid this rejection is a disturbing indication of the power of his fear. Nonetheless, understanding the murder as a way to avoid the intense physical pain of a shame response helps bring the act into focus.

Our national obsession with violent acts is largely superficial and appears to have spawned little more than a thirst for vengeance, as evidenced by our teeming prisons. Society needs to be protected as much as humanly possible from the violence that seems so prevalent at this time in our history. In order to understand the violence around us, however, we must confront the pain we cause each other. What is overlooked in all the media glare is a far more powerful need for personal acceptance, the only true antidote to the pain of rejection.

VII

THE SHAME RESPONSE AND CULTURAL DIFFERENCES

"For heaven's sake, tell me," said Thuillier to Tullia, the dancer, who happened to be calling at Madame Colleville's, "why don't women get attached to me? I'm not an Apollo Belevedere, but I'm no Vulcan either; I'm passably good-looking, I'm bright and I'm faithful..."
"Do you want to know the truth?"
said Tullia.
"Yes," said Beau Thuillier.
"Very good; although we can sometimes love a stupid man, we never love a fool."
That thrust was the end of Thuillier.

Honoré de Balzac [24]

Most societies use the threat of rejection, as well as some form of expulsion, such as imprisonment, as a means of maintaining law and order. In many ways, the threat of rejection forces us to learn to live together and thus provides a level of social conformity, perhaps even a certain harmony.

There is always the danger, however, that a minority claiming special status will use the threat of rejection to gain control of the majority. The National Socialists in Germany and the Bolsheviks in Russia ultimately gained complete control of their countries through violent repression, but they began with individual acts of rejection. Anyone unwilling to join with them was branded as an enemy.

Archaic Greece and early twentieth century Japan have been described as shame cultures, whereas the United States has been thought of as a guilt culture.[25] In the former societies, elaborate patterns of behavior evolved to protect individuals from random, unforeseen acts of rejection. As these patterns came to function more effectively with the passage of time, thus increasing the level of protection against rejection, they became powerful determinants of behavior and, in the case of Japan, extremely rigid. By contrast, such patterns in the United States are ill-defined, if present at all.

In Archaic Greece, unpardonable human errors, which would be grounds for absolute rejection of the individual, were attributed to *ate,* or a takeover of the person's mind by a divine being. It thus became the divine being who was responsible for the error, and not the person who erred. When a charioteer by the name of Automedon made the error of stepping down from his chariot during a battle, he explained his behavior as resulting from *ate.* When Glaucus, a soldier, swapped his gold armor for one made of bronze, he too, claimed *ate.*

E. R. Dodds, in his book "The Greeks and the Irrational" describes both of these events from the Iliad.[26] He explains that the use of *ate* was most likely to happen "when the acts in question are such as to cause acute shame to their author." In another context, he speaks of "unbearable feelings of shame." What may at first glance appear to be a quaint superstition, for few today believe in possession by a divine being, is actually a sophisticated defense mechanism against the pain of an intense rejection.

In early twentieth-century Japan, the dominant feature in the life of the individual was the risk of rejection. In her book "The Chrysanthemum and the Sword" Ruth Benedict writes of the Japanese man (and woman): "All his life ostracism is more dreaded than violence."[27] Benedict quotes from a book by Yoshio Markimo:

> I visited upon one of the missionaries in whom I had more confidence than any other. I told him my intention to go to America in hope that he might be able to give me some useful information. To my great disappointment, he exclaimed, "What, *you* are intending to go to America?" His wife was in the same room, and they both *sneered* at me! At the moment, I felt that all the blood in my head went down to my feet!
> Let me give you my definition of two words. Murderer: one who assassinates some human flesh. Sneerer: one who assassinates others' SOUL and *heart*.
> Soul and heart are far dearer than the flesh, therefore sneering is the worst crime. Indeed, that missionary and his wife tried to assassinate my *soul* and *heart*, and I had a great pain in my heart, which cried out, "Why you?"

Later in her book, Benedict suggests that the missionaries did not sneer at the young man but rather showed their incredulity at his wish, a penniless provincial youth, saying he would go to the United States to become an artist. Markimo's book was published in 1912.

In a book published in 1926 and quoted by Benedict, a Mrs. Sugimoto provides a description of a rejection in which the one rejecting has full knowledge of its consequences. Mrs. Sugimoto had studied with a Confucian scholar from the age of six.

Throughout my two-hour lesson, he never moved the slightest fraction of an inch except for his hands and his lips. And I sat before him on the matting in an equally correct and unchanging position. Once I moved. It was in the midst of a lesson. For some reason, I was restless and swayed my body slightly, allowing my folded knee to slip a little from the proper angle.

The faintest shade of surprise crossed my instructor's face; then, very quietly, he closed his book, saying gently, but with a stern air: "Little Miss, it is evident that your mental attitude today is not suited for study. You should retire to your room and meditate." My little heart was almost killed with shame. There was nothing I could do. I humbly bowed to the picture of Confucius and then to my teacher, and, backing respectfully from the room, I slowly went to my father to report as I always did, at the close of my lesson. Father was surprised, as the time was not yet up, and his unconscious remark, "How quickly you have done your work!" was like a death knell. The memory of that moment hurts like a bruise to this very day.

In early twentieth-century Japan, total conformity to rigid rules of etiquette provided the means for individuals to avoid experiencing rejection. When a person failed to conform, however, the result was exposure to a shame response so painful it will never be forgotten.

In contrast to Archaic Greece and early twentieth-century Japan, Americas patterns of behavior often fail to protect the individual from rejection. Until recently, widespread legally sanctioned segregation of African Americans was generally accepted. The rejection this entailed is obvious, but the pain of the shame response is not. If those rejected expressed anger, it was responded to with more anger. The anger was usually hidden, however, or at times displaced onto other African Americans. As to the pain of the shame response, it persists, and has caused long lasting consequences for individuals in the form of withdrawal, depression, and isolation.

In this country, Puritanism focused attention on guilt for committing a wrong and sanctioned rejection of those who did so. Patterns of protecting individuals from experiencing random acts of rejection have received little attention. Recently, the idea of shaming those who have been convicted of a crime has gained widespread attention. Should this practice gain currency, it promises that some who will be deeply pained will simply bide their time until an opportunity presents itself for them to displace their anger onto other victims.[28]

VIII

Healing

If you do not understand what is meant by acceptance in human relations, then approach a homeless man on the street when he is not begging. Ask him if he would be offended if you gave him the dollar you are holding in your hand. The look on his face, when he realizes you are asking for his approval, may well explain to you the meaning of acceptance.

Every day some of us will experience rejection and, if the rejection is significant, the shame response that ensues. Generally, when the pain is slight, it will be repressed or isolated, and it will be forgotten. When it persists, it may be possible to share the experience with trusted others. In doing so, we open up the possibility of understanding what occurred in a way that allows us to distance ourselves from it. Relief comes *only* if we are able to objectify the experience of rejection (i.e., objectify the objectification). It may become obvious, as we recount to another what has happened to us, that others were rejected at the same time and that we were not singled out as we had supposed. An awareness may arise in us in which it is clear that no rejection was ever intended. For those fortunate enough to have friends who can be counted on to side with us, or at least to hear us out, relief is possible. With relief, the pain subsides or disappears.

Healing is possible following an intensely painful shame response, but it is most difficult to achieve. We are human animals or, as one author has written, moral animals.[29] It is in our nature to keep intense shame responses a closely held secret. This secrecy extends to experiences of shame responses whether intense or not, but the more intense the shame response, the greater will be the perceived need for secrecy. Secrecy makes healing difficult, for without a sharing of the experience of rejection, it cannot be placed at a distance that allows it to be considered objectively.

No one is as critical of our own behavior as we ourselves. It is for this reason that many of us keep our painful experiences secret. The need for secrecy is based on the belief that everyone will be as rejecting of our behavior as we are. When we are rejected by a significant other for something we have said or done, the intensity of the shame response is supported by our own rejection. When we reject our own behavior, we can experience a shame response even when we are alone. Understanding that the human animal is hardly fully evolved and that all of us experience the pain of the shame response at one time or another may help us break through this culture of secrecy. It is a shared pain and, as such, a part of our humanity.

Just how difficult it is to experience healing, and thus find relief, is demonstrated by the following vignettes:

A. A professional woman, fired from her job in a prestigious governmental agency, finally was able to describe the intense physical pain she had endured because of the firing. She blurted out the word: "Terrible!" She said this after many hours of slow, difficult work.

When she began to describe her behavior that preceded her firing, she seemed to become convinced that the therapist would reject her as well. At that point, she terminated therapy.

B. A man who had experienced the intense physical pain of a shame response established the parameters of how therapy would be conducted. It was agreed that, if the pain became too intense as he worked through the events that occurred, he would say so and leave. It was also agreed that the frequency of the visits would be determined by him.

Within these guidelines, he was gradually able to process what had taken place. A milestone in his therapy was reached when he was able to say that both he and the man who rejected him knew of a deeper secret that was never mentioned between them, but that entailed the potential for an even greater rejection than that which had occurred. This point was reached after many months of slowly working through the events of what had been, for the patient, one of the most painful of life experiences.

C. A young woman explained that when she became dependent on a man who was her lover, she would find herself intruding more and more into his life. The intrusions occurred in ways that were most unwelcome and, when the man began to reject them, she became even more intrusive.

Over the course of therapy, she gradually saw that she began each relationship believing that she would be rejected. When she began to experience the rejection, whether real or perceived, the pain quickly became intolerable. At this point she would seek solace for the pain from her lover, but in ways that brought more rejection. When she finally saw the vicious circle she was trapped in, she haltingly sought solace elsewhere.

For a therapist, whatever his or her professional background may be, or just a deeply caring person, to help one heal following an intensely painful shame response requires great patience and, more especially, a deeply felt acceptance of the person. The challenge to deep acceptance lies in the ever present risk of experiencing rejection and, hence, pain. Our fear of rejection leaves so many of us confined to a narrow path of self-protection.

IX

ACCEPTANCE

And forget not that the earth delights to feel your bare feet and the winds long to play with your hair.

Kahlil Gibran [30]

The story of Adam and Eve's expulsion from the Garden of Eden dramatizes our inner conviction that we are somehow deserving of rejection. That an angel with a flaming sword is stationed at the gate only confirms this belief, as the angel is there to prevent our return.

Many have suffered what they perceive to be rejection at the hands of their parents, yet the experience of moving on from childhood, of growing up and leaving it behind, is hardly a consequence of parental rejection. Not surprisingly, however, people can confuse parental rejection with loss of childhood. In a similar fashion, we may have misinterpreted the story of Adam and Eve, which admits a second interpretation, one in which there is no rejection. Adam and Eve depart from the garden in order to go out into the world and experience it, to grow in understanding of it, and, most of all, to be challenged by it. This interpretation emphasizes growth and progress toward some ultimate destination.

This interpretation is not far fetched. Great Jewish[31] and Christian[32] mystics talk of seeing or entering an orchard, more often thought of by Christian mystics as a garden, that is of such incredible beauty that it cannot be described. What they clearly suggest is that it is worth expending all our life energy to reach it and that each of us in our own way, along our own unique path, may arrive at such a destination. In the Zohar,[33] considered to be a most sacred Jewish mystical text, it is taught that, as we strive to approach the divine, the light of the divine presence reaches down to surround us, to accept us. To abandon the notion of the descent from rejection is to acknowledge the ascent into acceptance.

In our daily lives, in our encounters with one another, the possibility that we may be seen as rejecting, particularly when we have no such intent, must be always in the forefront of our conscious awareness. If we need to confront someone about his behavior, we can do it in a way that allows him to experience acceptance and not rejection. For example, he should not be taken by surprise, but rather taken out of the earshot of others and helped to understand the problem his behavior has created for us. He needs to be helped to understand that he is not the problem, but his behavior is.

Men and women in positions of authority in every walk of life, whether it is in a maximum security prison, in a youth development center, or in a university classroom, must always be conscious of their power to cause pain in those under their authority. When they see someone respond in anger, blush or cry, they must realize that that person may be experiencing a shame response.

If we acknowledge the extent to which we reject one another, and how long the shame response has eluded us, it will be easy to feel that changing human behavior is next to impossible. The dream of a man who experienced a particularly painful shame response may provide encouragement. He was a veteran of the war in Vietnam, and reported a dream as follows:

> I was walking across a battlefield under a dark grey sky. There was no activity and no one to be seen anywhere. It was a sea of mud, shell holes filled with water, stumps of trees, and nothing else. Everything had been destroyed. It looked like a scene in France in the First World War. A passage appeared leading down into the earth and I followed it down. It came out into this beautiful, quiet place that was full of light. There were lovely gardens, trees, and open spaces surrounded by attractive buildings. There were groups of people standing about conversing with one another. They were very relaxed and obviously enjoying themselves. It was very quiet and everything was peaceful.
>
> I went over to a man standing at the edge of a group of people and asked him what they did about

rejection. He said there wasn't any, but there were movies about it from the past and I could view them if I was interested. But he reflected for a moment and said, it was not something I needed to do as I had come down from up above and seen all there was to see.

When he was asked about this dream several months after he recounted it, he could remember nothing about it.

X

Equality

I saw my Lord with the eye of the heart.
I asked Him: Who art thou? He answered:
Thou.

Mansur al Halaaj
— martyred 922 C. E. [34]

It is said that all men and women are born equal, yet the very family into which we are born is hierarchical. Year of birth determines the hierarchy of our relationships to one another, if nothing else. In addition, societal values of every kind are reflected in the family, and differences of gender, physical beauty, intelligence, personality, and personal wealth provide the framework for various hierarchies. Pressures mount throughout our lives to see some as superiors and others as inferiors. To believe that there are men and women who are our superiors or our inferiors means, at the very least, that we see ourselves as different from them.

A dissident Russian psychiatrist, Anatoly Koryagin, described a cafeteria in a factory East of the Ural Mountains in then Communist Russia. A small section of the cafeteria was walled off with cheap panelling. The area inside was no different than that outside except for the fact that inside a glass of water was set on each table with a single flower in it. This was the only benefit he was aware of that flowed from being a member of the Communist Party, namely the right to enter this area. Yet, according to what he knew, this small place was enough to maintain a rigid social hierarchy of those who belonged, who were accepted, and those who did not.[35]

In a hierarchical society, we reject those who are seen as inferiors out of fear that, otherwise, our own status will be lowered in the scale of things. All too often those rejected are rejected simply because they speak, dress or act differently from us and for no other reason. Much that leads to individuals being rejected is irrelevant at best, and outrageous at worst. (When those rejected show themselves, in response, to be destructive and ignorant of the rights of others, we find justification for our own rejection of them.)

Rejection based on hierarchy persists because of our need to see others as different from ourselves. To think otherwise might put *us* at risk of being rejected. The fear of the physical pain of the shame response is one factor which cements a hierarchical society in place.

Rabbi Luzzatto, writing in the first half of the Eighteenth Century, said that a soul enters the body in order to perfect itself through good deeds. This holds true for every being. Not for a few superior beings, but everyone.[36] To be a mechanical engineer or to be a mechanic both offer a chance for a person to work to the best of his or her ability. To see that a powerful engine is designed in the safest way possible or that a truck is repaired and does not break down in a winter storm are equally important tasks. Both the engineer and the mechanic are working to make life safer and more predictable. There is no reason to see one as inferior to the other unless there is a fear of rejection to contend with. To see another as having a choice in doing good by caring for others or not is a sufficient measure of any man or woman.

REFERENCES

1. Gilbert, M., *The First World War* (New York: Henry Holt, 1994) p. 228.
2. Ellis, J., *Eye-Deep in Hell* (Baltimore: Johns Hopkins University Press, 1989) p. 80.
3. Kundera, M., *Testaments Betrayed* (New York: Harper Collins, 1993) p. 263.
4. *Webster's Third New International Dictionary* (Springfield: G. and C. Merriman, 1986).
5. Freud, S., "The Interpretation of Dreams" In J. Strachey, Ed. and Trans., *The Standard Edition of the Complete Psychological Works of Sigmund Freud*, (London: Hogarth Press, Vols. 4 and 5, 1953, first published 1900).
6. Joyce, J., *Ulysses* (New York: The Modern Library, 1992, first published 1922).
7. Austen, J., *Emma* (New York and London: Penguin Books, 1996, first published 1816) p. 364.
8. Dickens, C., *Great Expectations* (New York and London: Penguin Books, 1985, first published 1860-61).
9. Shelley, M., *Frankenstein* (Berkeley and Los Angeles: University of California Press, 1994, first published 1818) p. 140.
10. Shakespeare, W., *The Tragedy of Hamlet, Prince of Denmark* (New Haven and London: Yale University Press, 1963, first published 1604).
11. Kundera, op. cit.
12. Darwin, C., *The Expression of Emotions in Man and Animals* (New York: Appleton and Co., 1873) p. 347.
13. *Webster's Third New International Dictionary*, op. cit.
14. Freud, S., "Three Essays on the Theory of Sexuality" In J. Strachey, Ed. and Trans., *The Standard Edition of the Complete Psychological Works of Sigmund Freud* (London: Hogarth Press, 1953, first published 1905, Vol. 7) p. 231.

15. Freud, S., "Mourning and Melancholia" In J. Strachey, Ed. and Trans., *The Standard Edition of the Complete Psychological Works of Sigmund Freud* (London: Hogarth Press., 1953, first published 1917, Vol. 14) p. 247.

16. Fenichel, O., *The Psychoanalytic Theory of Neurosis* (New York: Norton, 1945) p. 139.

17. Rizutto, A. M., "Shame in Psychoanalysis: The Function of Unconscious Fantasies" *International Journal of Psycho-Analysis* (72:297-312., 1991).

18. Dickens, C., op. cit. p. 92.

19. Thomas, H., "Experiencing a Shame Response as a Precursor to Violence" *Bulletin American Academy Psychiatry and Law* (23:587-593, 1995).

20. Meyer, M. (Translator), *The Gospel of Thomas: The Hidden Sayings of Jesus* (San Francisco: Harper, 1992) p. 35.

21. Shin, M., et. al., "Visual Imagery and Perception in Post Traumatic Stress Disorder" *Archives of General Psychiatry* (54:233-241, 1997).

22. Menninger, K., *The Crime of Punishment* (New York: Viking Press, 1968) p. 280.

23. Lewis, D., et. al., "Neuropsychiatric, Psychoeducational, and Family Characteristics of 14 Juveniles Condemned to Death in the United States" *American Journal of Psychiatry* (145:584-59, 1988).

24. Balzac, H., *The Petty Bourgeois* (Philadelphia: George Barrie and Son, 1897).

25. Benedict, R., *The Chrysanthemum and the Sword: Patterns of Japanese Culture* (New York: New American Library, 1974) p. 159.

26. Dodds, E., *The Greeks and the Irrational* (Berkeley and Los Angeles: University of California Press, 1951) pp. 4, 17.

27. Benedict, Op. cit. p. 25.

28. See, e.g., Arney, J., "Shame and Punishment" *The Virginia Pilot* (March 2, 1997) p. J1.

29. Wright, R., *The Moral Animal* (New York: Pantheon Books, 1994).

30. Gibran, K., *The Prophet* (New York: Alfred A. Knoph, 1985, first published, 1923).
31. Kaplan, A., *Meditation and Kaballah* (York Beach, Maine: Samuel Weiser, 1982).
32. Underhill, E., *Mysticism* (New York: New American Library, 1974, first published 1910).
33. Sperling, H., and Simon, M., (Translators) *The Zohar* (London and New York: The Soncino Press, 1984).
34. Stoddard, W., *Sufism* (New York: Paragon House, 1985).
35. Koryagin, A., (Personal Communication)
36. Luzzatto, M., *The Way of God* (Jerusalem and New York: Feldheim Publishers, 1988, written 1734).

A NOTE ABOUT THE TYPE

The typestyles used in this book are *Goudy Highlights* and *Berkeley Retrospective*. Both were based on designs created by typographer Frederic Goudy. *Berkeley* was designed by Goudy in 1938 for his friend at the University of California Press at Berkeley.

Layout and page design by Martha Wasik.